TRANSFORMED BY THE WORD

Devotion and Meditations

On Psalm 119

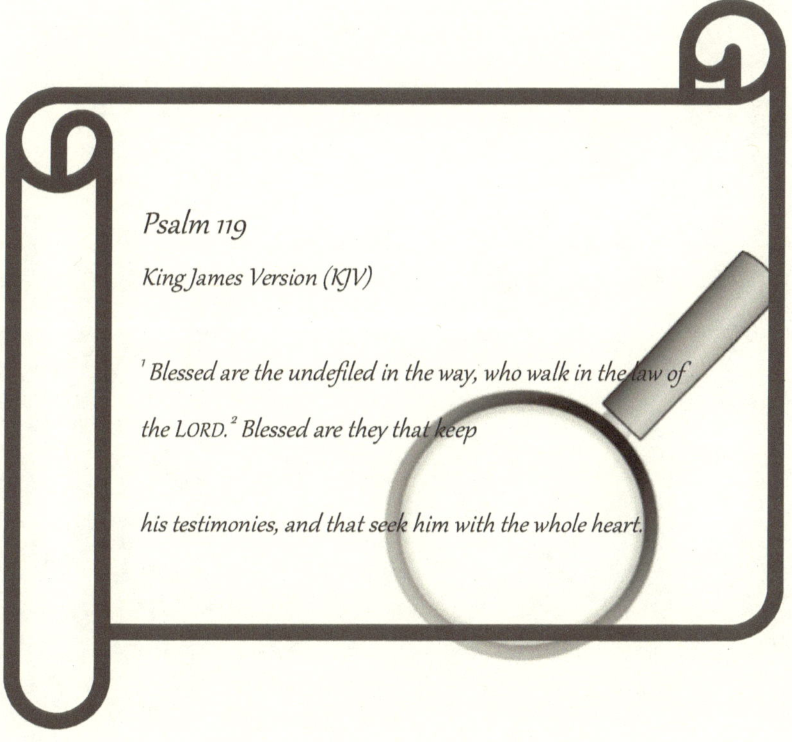

Pastor Willie Richardson

ISBN: 978-0-578-17143-2

DEDICATION

I dedicate this book to the memory of my parents James & Dora Richardson and to my spiritual father & mother in the gospel Pastor George and Mother Georgia Liggins.

To my wife Donsella (Donnie) of over forty years of marriage and our four wonderful children: Willie, Quentis, De'Vita and Evelyn. I love you all always.

To the Bread of Life Church family past and present, I thank God and you for allowing me to speak, preach and teach you week after week, WHAT TIME IS IT?

What time is it? Time to let there be light; what is light? Knowledge, order and understanding; where do we get that light? from the word of God.

CONTENTS

ACKNOWLEDGMENTS

I offer special thanks to my dear friend, Dr. Anthony Gantt, for always being an encouragement and excellent coach to me and anyone else that he can help discover the God-given gifts within.

I would also like to thank a precious saint and Sister, Dr. Mary Webster Moore, for all of her helpful advice, guidance, and editorial assistance, you are a jewel for real and I love you in Christ.

I want to give thanks to my nephew, Robert Richardson and niece, Fidelis Richardson for their help in revising and the publishing of this book on Amazon KDP. I love you and may God forever bless you for all your encouragements.

INTRODUCTION

Transformed by the word is a personal experience of over 37 years of salvation and love for the word of God. The things I will share in this book, are what I believe to be a revealed truth about the unchanging power of the Spoken, Written, and Living Word of God. First, I believe that God spoke the world into existence, just as it is recorded in Genesis chapter one. Secondly, I also believe that God inspired men to write His Word according to Romans 15:4 which say's:

"For whatsoever things were written aforetime were written for our learning, that we through patience and comfort of the scriptures might have hope".

But the revealed truth is that long before men wrote His Word on earth, God's Word was written before him in heaven for them that feared the Lord Malachi 3:16 reads

> ***Then they that feared the LORD spoke often one to another: and the LORD hearkened, and heard it, and a book of remembrance was written before him for them that feared the LORD, and that thought upon his name.***

What an awesome revelation, that God wrote His Word in heaven long before men were inspired to write his word on Earth. But think about it, God reveals to us in Jeremiah 3:5 that He knows us long before we are born. He knew and chose Jeremiah, Moses and every other writer of the Bible. The Apostle Paul says in Romans 15:4

For whatsoever things were written aforetime **(times pass)** ***were written for our learning, that we through patience and comfort of the scriptures might have hope.***

Lastly, the living Word of God (Jesus) was manifested in the flesh and dwelt among us as John1: 14 say,

"And the Word was made flesh, and dwelt among us, (and

we beheld his glory, the glory as of the only begotten of the Father,) full of grace and truth".

The power of the Word cannot be broken, as Jesus said in John 10:34-35

"Is it not written in your law, I said, ye are gods? If he called them gods, unto whom the word of God came, (and the scripture cannot be broken); how Say ye of him, whom the Father hath sanctified, and sent into the world, Thou blasphemes; because I said, I am the Son of God"?

However, the Word can change anything or anybody. Hebrews 4:12 says the Word of God is quick and powerful or (alive) and sharper than any two-edged sword. St. John the first chapter gives a clear and decisive picture of the presence and power of the Word when it says, "In the beginning was the Word and the Word was with God and the Word was God, the same was in the beginning with God All things (*all things*) were made by him and without him (the Word) was not anything made that was made" (vv.1-2) verse fourteen says: And the Word was made flesh, and dwelt among us, (and we beheld his glory, the glory as of the only begotten of the Father,) full of grace and truth.

I believe Psalm 119 gives a very powerful example of how the Word can change anything but it cannot *be* changed. Psalm 119 is unique and stands alone among the other 149 psalms, if for no other reason than it has 176 verses, holding the record of having more verses than any chapter in the bible. It also has many outstanding insights for anyone who loves to search the scriptures. Personally, one of the things that are so outstanding about this Psalm is that it is composed into twenty-two sections, each corresponding to the twenty-two letters of the Hebrew alphabet.

As we encounter this Psalm in most of our modern translations, each letter of the Hebrew alphabet separates the Psalm into stanzas of *eight verses*. Eight is said to be the number of renewal, new beginnings, or starting over. In music for example there are eight notes; Do, Re, Mi, Fa, So, La, Ti and then it starts over again with a higher Do. I believe Psalm 119, with purpose and guidance, has divided within it, twenty-two sets of eight verses each. I believe the bible reveals a deep sense of the significance of the number eight the number for renewal. For example, we read in Genesis chapter 6:11-13 the story of Noah and his family, a total of eight souls who were saved from the flood to renew and replenish the Earth. In the six hundredth year and second month of Noah's life, the seventeenth day of the month, the same day were all the fountains of the great deep broken up, and the windows of heaven were opened. And the rain was upon the earth forty days and forty nights. In the selfsame day entered Noah, and Shem, and Ham, and Japheth, the sons of Noah, and Noah's wife, and the three wives of his sons with them into the ark.

Another is David the eighth son of Jesse was anointed by Samuel the prophet to be King after Saul's disobedience II Samuel 16:10-13. It's Solomon King David's son who says, "a just man falls seven times, and rises up again". To rise again after seven falls would be eight. Proverbs 24:16. What I have discovered throughout the 176 verses is that there are eight words in each stanza of the KJV and other translations. Those words are:

1. Judgment(s)
2. Commandment(s)
3. Statute(s)
4. Law(s)
5. Precept(s)
6. Testimony (es)
7. Way(s)
8. Word(s)

When you replace the first seven word(s) mentioned above with the eighth one, WORD or WORDS, you'll get a delightfully pleasing insight of almost every verse in Psalm 119. Re-reading the verses with WORD inserted, gives them more of a personal feeling – a sense of "God-in-your-face" speaking directly to you. At times you may experience feelings of remorse and regret over shortcomings, but most of the time you should feel worshipful giving praise and thanksgiving for who God is.

At the end of each of the eight stanzas there will be an exercise for you to revisit the eight words within that stanza. For example: In verses 1-8 you'll find the words, way or ways, law, testimonies, precepts, statutes, commandments, and judgments. Pick a verse out of the eight and quote (*speak the word*) out loud or memorize it. Then write in short what you felt or what was brought to your remembrance after or during your reading of the eight verses. Was there a feeling of sadness, sorrow, or remorse, or was it joy, peace, praise and worship? Also you will find after reading about the spoken, written and living word an additional five-meditation verse that relate to each. Lastly, share with someone else what you have learned. This book will work well in a group or family Bible study.

May the Lord bless you as you discern the spoken, written, and living word of God and to know that, as he has spoken we should speak, as it is written we should write and as He is alive we shall live!

MY PERSONAL EXPERIENCE BEING TRANSFORMED BY THE WORD

Transformed by the Word is my testimony and revelation that anything and anybody can be transformed (changed) by the Word of God. That is the spoken, written and living word, in the person of Jesus Christ. My personal testimony began on January 6, 1975 at about 3am in the dining room of my parents' home. At that moment that morning at the dining room table, as my father read the Bible, I heard a voice say," Tell him you want to be saved". The voice said it three times. On that third time as my father was reading I opened my mouth and said "Dad I want to be saved". He stopped reading and looked up at me as though he was surprised, and asked, "what did you say" I answered again and said; "I want to be saved". With joy on his face he said, "Willie, you are saved right now by the confession of your own mouth." At that same instant my mother said to Dad "Let's pray for him" As they prayed and asked me to thank the Lord for saving me I felt the presence of the Lord as he filled my being with His love. I went to bed that morning and for the first time I experienced what I say often, and that is, that, "I go to sleep on my way to my pillow."

Later that same morning my mother called me from the basement, where I was staying, to come up stairs and eat breakfast. As I was coming up the stairs I heard a voice say, "You know you acted real strange last night" and I answered the voice and said," Sure did". But at that same instant I could hear my mother on the phone saying "Willie got saved last night thank you Jesus" When she said thank you Jesus I said "thank you Jesus" and couldn't stop, I ran back down the basement stairs and fell at the back of the bed with my hands lifted and tears rolling down my face. It was then and there that I was transformed by the power of the Holy Ghost, Glory to God. It happened just like the scriptures record in Acts chapter's 2, 10 and 19; I began to speak in unlearned tongues.

I am convinced that it was this experience that enabled me to give up the many vices that had me bound and it agrees with the Word of God that says in II Corinthians 5:17 "If any man be in Christ he is a new creature old things are passed away; behold all things are become new." My testimony is this; from that day to this day I have been free from the powers of alcohol, drugs and the cigarette habit, my answer to how it happened is found in the Word of God that says, "But ye shall receive power after that the Holy Ghost is come upon you" Acts 1:8a. . I can truly say that I have been kept and led by the Holy Ghost all my new born again life. The transforming Word of God says it this way; as many as are led by the Spirit of God they are the sons of God.

1

ALEPH

Psalms 119 1:8

Discuss / Meditate

Keepers of God's Word

Those that keep God's word will read it, remember it, study it and obey it. Keepers of God's word speak, seek, sing and pray it. Psalm 51:6 says, "Behold, thou desirest truth in the inward parts: and in the hidden part thou shalt make me to know wisdom". Timothy was exhorted by the Apostle Paul to: "Meditate on these things (the Word of God), give thyself wholly to them; that thy profiting (worth and growth) may appear (be seen or apparent) to all."(Timothy 4:15)

Read each verse and transform it by the (WORD)

1 Blessed *are* the undefiled in the **word,** who walk in the **word** of the LORD.
2 Blessed *are* they that keep his **words**, *and that* seek him with the whole
heart. **3** They also do no iniquity: they walk in his **words. 4** Thou hast
commanded *us* to keep thy **words** diligently. **5** O that my **words** were
directed to keep thy **words.6** Then shall I not be ashamed, when I have
respect unto all thy **words. 7** I will praise thee with uprightness of heart,
when I shall have learned thy righteous **words**. **8** I will keep thy **words** O
forsake me not utterly.

Study Guide:
Write the words that were transformed by the Word?

1.________ 4.__________ 7.__________
2.________ 5.__________ 8.__________
3.________ 6.__________

Choose a memory verse

Psalm119:

____
____
____
____
____
____
____
____

Which verse challenged or blessed you after being transformed? Explain

____
____
____
____
____
____
____
____
____

2

ב

BETH

Psalms 119 9-16

Discuss / Meditate

The Fruit of God's Word

Will produce godly character traits in the believer; In Galatians 5:22 the Apostle Paul reveal's that the character traits and attributes of the Spirit of God, are love, joy, peace, longsuffering, gentleness, goodness, faith, meekness and temperance, against such it says there is no law (barrier, limitation or boundaries). Jesus reminds us that a tree is known by its fruit; read St. Matthew 7:20-33 and St. John 15:1-5

Read each verse and transform it by the (WORD)

9 Wherewithal shall a young man cleanse his **word**? By taking heed *thereto*
according to thy **word.** **10** With my whole heart have I sought thee: O let me not
wander from thy **words.** **11** Thy **word** have I hid in mine heart, that I might not sin
against thee. **12** Blessed *art* thou, O LORD: teach me thy **words.** **13**With my lips
have I declared all the **words** of thy mouth. **14** I have rejoiced in the **Word** of thy
words, as *much as* in all riches. **15** I will meditate in thy **words,** and have respect
unto thy **words.**16 I will delight myself in thy **words:** I will not forget thy **word.**

Study Guide:
Write the words that were transformed by the Word?

1.________ 4.___________ 7.___________
2.________ 5.___________ 8.___________
3.________ 6.___________

Choose a memory verse

Psalm119:

____
____
____
____
____
____
____
____

Which verse challenged or blessed you after being transformed? Explain

____
____
____
____
____
____
____
____
____

3

ג

Gimel

Psalms 119:17-24

Discuss / Meditate

Eyes to See God's Word

In order for a person to see (understand) Gods Word they must first be born again St. John 3:3
The Word of God says that if the gospel is hid it is hid from them that are lost whom the god of this world (the devil) has blinded their minds (II Corinthians 4:3-4). But for the believer Paul prays in Ephesians 1:18 that the eyes of our understanding would be enlightened.

Read each verse and transform it by the (WORD)

17 Deal bountifully with thy servant, *that* I may live, and keep thy **word.**
18 Open thou mine eyes, that I may behold wondrous things out of thy
word. **19** I *am* a stranger in the earth: hide not thy **words** from me. **20** My
soul breaketh for the longing *that it hath* unto thy **words** at all times.
21 Thou hast rebuked the proud *that are* cursed, which do err from thy
words.22 Remove from me reproach and contempt; for I have kept thy
words. **23** Princes also did sit *and* speak against me: *but* thy servant did
meditate in thy **words.24** Thy **words** also *are* my delight *and* my
counselors.

Study Guide:
Write the words that were transformed by the Word?

1.________ 4.___________ 7.___________
2.________ 5.___________ 8.___________
3.________ 6.___________

Choose a memory verse

Psalm119:

____
____
____
____
____
____
____
____

Which verse challenged or blessed you after being transformed? Explain

____
____
____
____
____
____
____
____

4

ד

Daleth

Psalms 119:25-32

Discuss / Meditate

Praying to Understand God's Word

Praying simply means; talking to God about his Word, which develops an intimate relationship with him. Scriptures say:" Men ought always to pray and not faint."(Luke 18:1) "Pray without ceasing" (I Thessalonians 5:17) Philippians 4:6 says" Be careful for nothing; but in everything by prayer and supplication with thanksgiving let your requests be made known unto God."

Read each verse and transform it by the (WORD)

25My soul cleaveth unto the dust: quicken thou me according to thy **word.** **26** I
have declared my **words,** and thou heardest me: teach me thy **words.** **27** Make me
to understand the **Word** of thy **word:** so shall I talk of thy wondrous works. **28** My
soul melteth for heaviness: strengthen thou me according unto thy **word.**
29 Remove from me the **word** of lying: and grant me thy word graciously. **30** I
have chosen the **word** of truth: thy **words** have I laid *before me.* **31** I have stuck
unto thy **words:** O LORD, put me not to shame. **32** I will run to the **Word** of thy
words, when thou shalt enlarge my heart.

Study Guide:
Write the words that were transformed by the Word?

1.________ 4.__________ 7.__________
2.________ 5.__________ 8.__________
3.________ 6.__________

Choose a memory verse

Psalm119:

____
____
____
____
____
____
____
____

Which verse challenged or blessed you after being transformed? Explain

____
____
____
____
____
____
____
____
____

5

ה

He

Psalms 119:33-40

Discuss / Meditate

Living by God’s Word

We learn that we must surrender, submit, sacrifice and yield ourselves to God through his written Word. Romans 12:1-2 says: “I beseech you therefore, brethren, by the mercies of God, that ye present your bodies a living sacrifice, holy, acceptable unto God, which is your reasonable service. And be not conformed to this world: but be ye transformed by the renewing of your mind, that ye may prove what is that good, and acceptable, and perfect, will of God”

Read each verse and transform it by the (WORD)

33 Teach me, O LORD, the **Word** of thy **words**; and I shall keep it *unto* the end.
34 Give me understanding, and I shall keep thy **word**; yea, I shall observe it with
my whole heart. **35** Make me to go in the path of thy **words**; for therein do I
delight. **36** Incline my heart unto thy **words,** and not to covetousness. **37** Turn
away mine eyes from beholding vanity; *and* quicken thou me in thy **word. 38**
Establish thy **word** unto thy servant, who *is devoted* to thy fear. **39** Turn away my
reproach, which I fear: for thy **words** *are* good. **40** Behold, I have longed after thy
words quicken me in thy righteousness.

Study Guide:
Write the words that were transformed by the Word?

1.________ 4.__________ 7.__________
2.________ 5.__________ 8.__________
3.________ 6.__________

Choose a memory verse

Psalm119:

____
____
____
____
____
____
____
____

Which verse challenged or blessed you after being transformed? Explain

____
____
____
____
____
____
____
____

6

ו

Vav

Psalms 119:41-48

Discuss / Meditate

Salvation through God's Word

Jesus Christ brought us salvation as the living Word Acts 4:12 says: "Neither is there salvation in any other: for there is none other name under heaven given among men, whereby we must be saved. St. John 1:14 says, "The Word was made flesh and dwelt among us, (and we beheld his glory, the glory as of the only begotten of the Father,) full of grace and truth.

Read each verse and transform it by the (WORD)

41 Let thy mercies come also unto me, O LORD, *even* thy salvation,
according to thy **word.** **42** So shall I have wherewith to answer him that
reproacheth me: for I trust in thy **word.** **43** And take not the **word** of truth
utterly out of my mouth; for I have hoped in thy **words.** **44** So shall I keep
thy **words** continually forever and ever. **45** And I will walk at liberty: for I
seek thy **words**. **46** I will speak of thy **words** also before kings, and will not
be ashamed. **47** And I will delight myself in thy **words, which** I have loved.
48 My hands also will I lift up unto thy **words**, which I have loved; and I
will meditate in thy **words.**

Study Guide:
Write the words that were transformed by the Word?

1.________ 4.__________ 7.__________
2.________ 5.__________ 8.__________
3.________ 6.__________

Choose a memory verse

Psalm119:

____
____
____
____
____
____
____
____

Which verse challenged or blessed you after being transformed? Explain

____
____
____
____
____
____
____
____
____

7

ז

Zayin

Psalms 119:49-56

Discuss / Meditate

Comfort in God's Word

Jesus promises the disciples in St. John 14:17, "I will not leave you comfortless;" this same promise is for us today. II Corinthians 1:3-4 says: "Blessed be God, even the Father of our Lord Jesus Christ, the Father of mercies, and the God of all comfort; Who comforteth us in all our tribulation, that we may be able to comfort them which are in any trouble, by the comfort wherewith we ourselves are comforted of God"

Read each verse and transform it by the (WORD)

49 Remember the **word** unto thy servant, upon which thou hast caused me to hope.
50 This *is* my comfort in my affliction: for thy **word** hath quickened me. **51** The
proud have had me greatly in derision: *yet* have I not declined from thy **word**. **52** I
remembered thy **words** of old, O LORD; and have comforted myself. **53** Horror
hath taken hold upon me because of the wicked that forsake thy **word.** **54** Thy
words have been my songs in the house of my pilgrimage. **55** I have remembered
thy name, O LORD, in the night, and have kept thy **word.** **56** This I had, because I
kept thy **words.**

Study Guide:
Write the words that were transformed by the Word?

1.________ 4.___________ 7.___________
2.________ 5.___________ 8.___________
3.________ 6.___________

Choose a memory verse

Psalm119:

____
____
____
____
____
____
____
____

Which verse challenged or blessed you after being transformed? Explain

____
____
____
____
____
____
____
____

8

Cheth

Psalm 119:57-64

Discuss / Meditate

God's Word, Our Portion

God is our portion our part our fill or our measure: St Matthews 5:6 says: "Blessed are they which do hunger and thirst after righteousness for they shall be filled." Psalm 142:5 says: "I cried unto thee, O LORD: I said, Thou art my refuge and my portion in the land of the living. The Apostle Paul declares in Philippians 4:19 "But my God shall supply all your need according to his riches in glory by Christ Jesus"

Read each verse and transform it by the (WORD)

57 *Thou art* my portion, O LORD: I have said that I would keep thy **words.** **58** I
entreated thy favour with *my* whole heart: be merciful unto me according to thy
word. **59** I thought on my **words,** and turned my feet unto thy **words.** **60** I made
haste, and delayed not to keep thy **words.** **61** The bands of the wicked have robbed
me: *but* I have not forgotten thy **word.** **62** At midnight I will rise to give thanks
unto thee because of thy righteous **words.** **63** I *am* a companion of all them that
fears thee, and of them that keep thy **words** **64** the earth, O LORD, is full of thy
mercy: teach me thy **words**.

Study Guide:
Write the words that were transformed by the Word?

1.________ 4.___________ 7.___________
2.________ 5.___________ 8.___________
3.________ 6.___________

Choose a memory verse

Psalm119:

____
____
____
____
____
____
____
____

Which verse challenged or blessed you after being transformed? Explain

____
____
____
____
____
____
____
____
____

TRANSFORMED BY THE SPOKEN WORD

Genesis chapter one says: "In the beginning God created the heaven and the earth. And the earth was without form, and void; and darkness was upon the face of the deep. And the Spirit of God moved upon the face of the water. And God said, "Let there be light and there was light" and there was light.

. God spoke everything into existence, both the seen and the unseen. Hebrews 11:3 says: "Through faith we understand that the worlds were framed by the Word of God, so that things which are seen were not made of things which do appear. God created all things by the word of his mouth" and I believe that we also must be careful of the words we speak, because we are made in God's image and after his likeness we are transformed by his Word but I also believe the words we speak, we also can transform others' lives by what we speak. You may have heard it said that "sticks and stones may break my bones but words will never hurt me" But that's not true, words can hurt long after the wounds of sticks and stones have healed. Proverbs 18:21 says, "Death and life *are* in the power of the tongue (the spoken word) and they that love it shall eat the fruit thereof." In other words our words are seeds, which will produce and manifest the harvest we continually love to speak. Jesus said in St. Matthews 12:37 "that by a man's words he will be justified and by his words he will be condemned." The power is not in what we thinking but in what we say.

When God made man he spoke and said "let us make man in our image after our likeness" Genesis 1:26. In this statement God reveals something of himself, by using the plural words us and our (let <u>us</u> make man in <u>our</u> image. Which I believe reveals the Trinity or the Godhead; The Father, Son (Word) and the Holy Ghost. I John 4:7 says: "For there are three that bear record in heaven, the Father, the Word, and the Holy Ghost: and these three are one". When God created man He made him triune shaped him first from the dust of the ground which is the (body or flesh) second He bereaved into man's body (nostrils) the breath of life (spirit) which is His Spirit and thirdly man became a living soul (an eternal being) Genesis2: 7. Man is a spirit with a soul that lives in a body.

Another manifestation of man being threefold is when God put him to sleep and took out of man (the specie) a rib and create woman (the gender) and told them to be fruitful and to multiply reproduce themselves in the earth. Genesis 1:28 in other words God was saying go have some babies. Think about this' God took out of himself (one) to made man (two) he took out of man and made the woman (three) he took out of the woman and made a child.

And the LORD God caused a deep sleep to fall upon Adam, and he slept: and he took one of his ribs, and closed up the flesh instead thereof; And the rib, which the LORD God had taken from man, made he a woman, and brought her unto the man. And Adam said, "This is now bone of my bones, and flesh of my flesh: she shall be called Woman, because she was taken out of Man". Therefore shall a man leave his father and his mother, and shall cleave unto his wife: and they shall be one flesh.

Ephesians 5:31 says:" For this cause shall a man leave his father and mother, and shall be joined unto his wife, and *they two shall be one flesh".*

The Spoken Word of God said "Let us make man in our image after our likeness." God said it I believe it and that settles it.

Scriptures for Meditation On the Spoken Word

1. Numbers 23:19 God is not a man that he should lie; neither the son of man that he should repent: hath he said, and shall he not do it? or hath he spoken, and shall he not make it good?

2. Isaiah 45:19 I have not spoken in secret, in a dark place of the earth: I said not unto the seed of Jacob, Seek ye me in vain: I the LORD speak righteousness, I declare things that are right.

3. Isaiah 48:16Come ye near unto me, hear ye this; I have not spoken in secret from the beginning;
from the time that it was, there am I: and now the Lord GOD, and his Spirit, hath sent me.

4. Isaiah 55:11, So shall my word be that goeth forth out of my mouth: it shall not return unto me void, but it shall accomplish that which I please, and it shall prosper in the thing whereto I sent it.

5. Psalm 62:11 God hath spoken once; twice have I heard this; that power belongeth unto God.

9

TETH

Psalms 119:65-72

Discuss / Meditate

God's Word Taught through Affliction

No one wants or looks forward to affliction be it mental, physical or spiritual; but sense we all must live with affliction God somehow uses it to Grow and mature us in him. Psalm 34:19 says, "Many are the afflictions of the righteous: but the LORD delivereth him out of them all. "Job is one of our greater examples and he said: I have heard of thee by the hearing of the ear: but now mine eye seeth thee. Job 42:5

Read each verse and transform it by the (WORD)

65 Thou hast dealt well with thy servant, O LORD, according unto thy **word.**
66 Teach me good **word** and knowledge: for I have believed thy **words**. **67** Before
I was afflicted I went astray: but now have I kept thy **word**. **68** Thou *art* good, and
doest good; teach me thy **words**. **69**The proud have forged a lie against me: *but* I
will keep thy **words** with *my* whole heart. **70** Their heart is as fat as grease; *but* I
delight in thy **word.** **71** *It is* good for me that I have been afflicted; that I might
learn thy **words**. **72** The **word** of thy mouth *is* better unto me than thousands of
gold and silver.

Study Guide:
Write the words that were transformed by the Word?

1.________ 4.__________ 7.__________
2.________ 5.__________ 8.__________
3.________ 6.__________

Choose a memory verse

Psalm119:

____
____
____
____
____
____
____
____

Which verse challenged or blessed you after being transformed? Explain

____
____
____
____
____
____
____
____
____

10

י

YOD

Psalm 119:73-80

Discuss / Meditate

Confidence in God's Word

Confidence in God's Word is to have faith in his word St. Mark 11:22 says: And Jesus answering saith unto them, Have faith in God. Hebrews 11:6 says: But without faith it is impossible to please him: for he that cometh to God must believe that he is, and that he is a rewarder of them that diligently seek him. One of my favorite scriptures says: Cast not away therefore your confidence, which hath great recompense of reward. For ye have need of patience, that, after ye have done the will of God, ye might receive the promise. Hebrews 10:35-36

Read each verse and transform it by the (WORD)

73 Thy hands have made me and fashioned me: give me understanding, that I may learn thy
words. **74**They that fear thee will be glad when they see me; because I have hoped in thy
word. 75 I know, O LORD, that thy **words** *are* right, and *that* thou in faithfulness hast
afflicted me. **76** Let, I pray thee, thy merciful kindness be for my comfort, according to thy
word unto thy servant. **77** Let thy tender mercies come unto me, that I may live: for thy
word *is* my delight. **78** Let the proud be ashamed; for they dealt perversely with me
without a cause: *but* I will meditate in thy **words. 79** Let those that fear thee turn unto me,
and those that have known thy **words.80** Let my heart be sound in thy **words;** that I be not
ashamed.

Study Guide:
Write the words that were transformed by the Word?

1.________ 4.___________ 7.___________
2.________ 5.___________ 8.___________
3.________ 6.___________

Choose a memory verse

Psalm119:

____
____
____
____
____
____
____
____

Which verse challenged or blessed you after being transformed? Explain

____
____
____
____
____
____
____
____
____

11

ךכ

CAPH

Psalms 119:81-88

Discuss / Meditate

Trust in God's Word

Trust in God's Word means: It may not happen right away, but you will rest and rely without care in his word. Trust in the LORD with all thine heart; and lean not unto thine own understanding. In all thy ways acknowledge him, and he shall direct thy paths. Proverbs 3:5-6 also Proverbs says: Every word of God is pure: he is a shield unto them that put their trust in him.

Read each verse and transform it by the (WORD)

81 My soul fainteth for thy salvation: *but* I hope in thy **word.** **82** Mine eyes fail for
thy **word,** saying, When wilt thou comfort me? **83** For I am become like a bottle in
the smoke; *yet* do I not forget thy **words.** **84** How many *are* the days of thy
servant? When wilst thou execute **word** on them that persecute me? **85** The proud
have dug pits for me, which *are* not after thy **word.** **86** All thy **words** *are* faithful:
they persecute me wrongfully; help thou me. **87** They had almost consumed me
upon earth; but I forsook not thy **words.** **88** Quicken me after thy loving kindness;
so shall I keep the **word** of thy mouth.

Study Guide:
Write the words that were transformed by the Word?

1.________ 4.___________ 7.___________
2.________ 5.___________ 8.___________
3.________ 6.___________

Choose a memory verse

Psalm119:

____
____
____
____
____
____
____
____

Which verse challenged or blessed you after being transformed? Explain

____
____
____
____
____
____
____
____
____

12

ל

LAMED

Psalms 119:89-96

Discuss / Meditate

God's Unchangeable Word

God's Word is immutable meaning not subject to change. Malachi 3: 6 says, " For I am the LORD, I change not; therefore ye sons of Jacob are not consumed." For an example to Abraham God promised He'd bless him and his seed and through his seed all the families of the earth would be blessed. Genesis 12:2-3

Read each verse and transform it by the (WORD)

89 Forever, O LORD, thy word is settled in heaven. **90** Thy faithfulness *is* unto all
generations: thou hast established the earth, and it abideth. **91** They continue this
day according to thine **words:** for all *are* thy servants. **92** Unless thy **word** *had*
been my delights, I should then have perished in mine affliction. **93** I will never
forget thy **words** for with them thou hast quickened me. **94** I *am* thine, save me; for
I have sought thy **words**. **95** The wicked have waited for me to destroy me: *but* I
will consider thy **words.** **96** I have seen an end of all perfection: *but* thy **word** *is*
exceeding broad.

Study Guide:
Write the words that were transformed by the Word?

1.________ 4.___________ 7.___________
2.________ 5.___________ 8.___________
3.________ 6.___________

Choose a memory verse

Psalm119:

____
____
____
____
____
____
____
____

Which verse challenged or blessed you after being transformed? Explain

____
____
____
____
____
____
____
____
____

13

ם מ

MEM

Psalms 119:97-104

Discuss / Meditate

The Love of God's Word

Jesus said: If ye" love me, keep my commandments." "He that hath my commandments, and keepeth them, he it is that loveth me: and he that loveth me shall be loved of my Father, and I will love him, and will manifest myself to him." "If a man love me, he will keep my words: and my Father will love him, and we will come unto him, and make our abode with him". St. John 14:15; 21; 23

Read each verse transformed by the (WORD)

97 O how love I thy **word!** It *is* my meditation all the day. **98** Thou through thy
words hast made me wiser than mine enemies: for they *are* ever with me. **99** I
have more understanding than all my teachers: for thy **words** *are* my meditation.
100 I understand more than the ancients, because I keep thy **words.** **101** I have
refrained my feet from every evil **word,** that I might keep thy **word**. **102** I have not
departed from thy **words**: for thou hast taught me. **103** How sweet are thy **words**
unto my taste! *Yea, sweeter* than honey to my mouth! **104** Through thy **words** I get
understanding: therefore I hate every false **word.**

Study Guide:
Write the words that were transformed by the Word?

1.________ 4.__________ 7.__________
2.________ 5.__________ 8.__________
3.________ 6.__________

Choose a memory verse

Psalm119:

____
____
____
____
____
____
____
____

Which verse challenged or blessed you after being transformed? Explain

____
____
____
____
____
____
____
____
____

14

ן נ

NUN

Psalms 119:105-112

Discuss / Meditate

God’s Word a Guide Forever

God’s Word is a Guide Forever: Jesus (the living Word) promised he’d send the guide called the Comforter, Holy Ghost, Spirit of truth St. John 16:13; 15 declares: “Howbeit when he, the Spirit of truth, is come, he will guide you into all truth: for he shall not speak of himself; but whatsoever he shall hear, that shall he speak: and he will show you things to come.” “All things that the Father hath are mine: therefore said I, that he shall take of mine, and shall show it unto you.” Read also John 14:16-17; 26 Thanks be to God the Holy Ghost is our guide today.

Read each verse and transform it by the (WORD)

105 Thy **word** *is* a lamp unto my feet, and a light unto my path. **106** I have sworn,
and I will perform *it*, that I will keep thy righteous **words**. **107** I am afflicted very
much: quicken me, O LORD, according unto thy **word.** **108** Accept, I beseech thee,
the freewill offerings of my mouth, O LORD, and teach me thy **words**. **109** My soul
is continually in my hand: yet do I not forget thy **word.** **110** The wicked have laid a
snare for me: yet I erred not from thy **words.** **111** Thy **words** have I taken as a
heritage forever: for they *are* the rejoicing of my heart. **112** I have inclined mine
heart to perform thy **words** always *even unto* the end.

Study Guide:
Write the words that were transformed by the Word?

1.________ 4.__________ 7.__________
2.________ 5.__________ 8.__________
3.________ 6.__________

Choose a memory verse

Psalm119:

____
____
____
____
____
____
____
____

Which verse challenged or blessed you after being transformed? Explain

____
____
____
____
____
____
____
____
____

TRANSFORMED BY THE WRITTEN WORD

In Malachi 3:16 there is a mystery revealed concerning the written word of God which says: "Then they that feared the LORD spoke often one to another: and the LORD hearkened, and heard *it*, and a book of remembrance was written before him for them that feared the LORD, and that thought upon his name."

My interpretation of this verse is: there was a time in the pass before men started writing that those that feared the LORD meaning those that honored and reverenced the LORD. "Spoke often one to another" they often talked and testified telling their story one to another of how good the LORD had been and how he had worked in their lives. "And the LORD hearkened, and heard it," and the LORD listen and acknowledge them, "and a book of remembrance was written before him for them that feared the LORD. And a memorial book that could be remembered was written in the presence of the LORD for them that honored and reverenced his name. Now before you reject this remember God is not like man he knows the end from the beginning He says:" Remember the former things of old: for I am God, and there is none else; I am God, and there is none like me, Declaring the end from the beginning, and from ancient times the things that are not yet done, saying, My counsel shall stand, and I will do all my pleasure" (Isaiah 46:9-10).

The sixty-sixth books of the bible that we read today, I believe are the written Words of God. I'm not saying that these are the only written Word's of God because John 21:25 declares: "And there are also many other things which Jesus did, the which, if they should be written every one, I suppose that even the world itself could not contain the books that should be written." Paul said in Romans 15:4 that "whatsoever was written aforetime is written for our learning that we through patience and comfort of the scriptures might have hope."

There are many ways to be transformed by the written Word of God but three I believe are imperative. They are:

1.To Study

2.To Meditate and

3.To Speak

First, we can be transformed by the Study of the written Word, the Apostle Paul told Timothy to: "study to show thy self approved unto God a workmen that need not to be ashamed rightly dividing the Word of truth."(II Timothy 2:15) Secondly, we can be transformed by the written Word through Meditating and committing it to memory, Paul exhorts Timothy to "Meditate upon these things; give thyself wholly to them; that thy profiting may appear to all."(I Timothy 4:15) Thirdly, the written Word of God can transform us by speaking it. Romans 10:8-10 says: But what saith it? The word is nigh thee, even in thy mouth, and in thy heart: that is, the word of faith, which we preach; That if thou shalt confess with thy mouth the Lord Jesus, and shalt believe in thine heart that God hath raised him from the dead, thou shalt be saved. For with the heart man believeth unto righteousness; and with the mouth confession is made unto salvation.

Scripture for Meditation On the Written Word

1. Habakkuk 2:2 And the LORD answered me, and said, Write the vision, and make it plain upon tables, that he may run that readeth it.

2. Romans 15:4 for whatsoever things were written aforetime were written for our learning, that we through patience and comfort of the scriptures might have hope.

3. Proverb 3:3 Let not mercy and truth forsake thee: bind them about thy neck; write them upon the table of thine heart:

4. Jeremiah 30:2 Thus speaketh the LORD God of Israel, saying, Write thee all the words that I have spoken unto thee in a book.

5. Revelation 1:19 Write the things which thou hast seen, and the things which are, and the things which shall be hereafter;

15

SAMECH

Discuss / Meditate

Psalms 119:113-120

God's Word a Hiding Place

The Secret place to getaway Psalm 32:7 says: Thou art my hiding place; thou shalt preserve me from trouble; thou shalt compass me about with songs of deliverance. Selah. Psalm 91:1 says: He that dwelleth in the secret place of the most High shall abide under the shadow of the Almighty.

Read each verse and transform it by the (WORD)

113 I hate *vain* thoughts: but thy **word** do I love. **114** Thou *art* my hiding place and
my shield: I hope in thy **word.** **115** Depart from me, ye evildoers: for I will keep
the **words** of my God. **116** Uphold me according unto thy **word that** I may live:
and let me not be ashamed of my hope. **117** Hold thou me up, and I shall be safe:
and I will have respect unto thy **words** continually. **118** Thou hast trodden down
all them that err from thy **words** for their deceit *is* falsehood. **119** Thou putteth
away all the wicked of the earth *like* dross: therefore I love thy **words.** **120** My
flesh trembleth for fear of thee; and I am afraid of thy **words.**

Study Guide:
Write the words that were transformed by the Word?

1.________ 4.__________ 7.__________
2.________ 5.__________ 8.__________
3.________ 6.__________

Choose a memory verse

Psalm119:

____
____
____
____
____
____
____
____

Which verse challenged or blessed you after being transformed? Explain

____
____
____
____
____
____
____
____
____

16

ע

AIN

Psalms 119:121-128

Discuss / Meditate

Believers Love God's Word

Job declared his love of Gods Word: My foot hath held his steps, his way **(word)** have I kept, and not declined. Neither have I gone back from the commandment **(word)** of his lips; I have esteemed the words of his mouth more than my necessary food. (Job 23:11-12). Jesus said: He that hath my commandments **(word),** and keepeth them, he it is that loveth me: and he that loveth me shall be loved of my Father, and I will love him, and will manifest myself to him. (St. John 14:21) Just as physical food sustains the body so does the Word of God sustain the spirit and soul of the believer.

Read each verse and transform it by the (WORD)

121 I have done **word** and justice: leave me not to mine oppressors. **122** Be surety
for thy servant for good: let not the proud oppress me. **123** Mine eyes fail for thy
salvation, and for the **word** of thy righteousness. **124** Deal with thy servant
according unto thy mercy, and teach me thy **words**. **125** I *am* thy servant; give me
understanding, that I may know thy **words.** **126** *It is* time for *thee*, LORD, to work:
for they have made void thy **word**. **127** Therefore I love thy **words** above gold;
yea, above fine gold. **128** Therefore I esteem all *thy* **words** *concerning* all *things to be* right; *and* I hate every false **word.**

Study Guide:
Write the words that were transformed by the Word?

1.________	4.___________	7.___________
2.________	5.___________	8.___________
3.________	6.___________	

Choose a memory verse

Psalm119:

____
____
____
____
____
____
____
____

Which verse challenged or blessed you after being transformed? Explain

____
____
____
____
____
____
____
____
____

17

PE

ף פּ

Psalms 119:129-136

Discuss / Meditate

God's Word gives Knowledge Order and Understanding

Let me share with you some principles of God's Word giving; knowledge, order and understanding. Consider this: God's Word provides the (knowledge) of knowing how to do what God desire, the order of God's Word (wisdom) reveals what we should or shouldn't do, while the understanding of God's Word teaches when we should do it. I'll go into this with more detail in my book called "**Let there be Light**"

Read each verse and transform it by the (WORD)

129 Thy **words** *are* wonderful: therefore doth my soul keep them. **130** The entrance of thy
words giveth light; it giveth understanding unto the simple. **131** I opened my mouth, and
panted: for I longed for thy **words**.
132 Look thou upon me, and be merciful unto me, as thou usest to do unto those that love
thy name. **133** Order my steps in thy **word**: and let not any iniquity have dominion over
me. **134** Deliver me from the oppression of man: so will I keep thy **words.** **135** Make thy
face to shine upon thy servant; and teach me thy **words.** **136** Rivers of waters run down
mine eyes, because they keep not thy **word.**

Study Guide:
Write the words that were transformed by the Word?

1.________ 4.__________ 7.__________
2.________ 5.__________ 8.__________
3.________ 6.__________

Choose a memory verse

Psalm119:

____
____
____
____
____
____
____
____

Which verse challenged or blessed you after being transformed? Explain

____
____
____
____
____
____
____
____
____

18

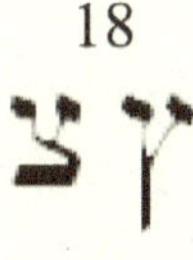

TZADDI

Psalms 119:137-144

Discuss / Meditate

God's Word is true

God's Word is true whether it's His spoken, written or living Word: You can depend, rely and trust in God's Word. Isaiah 55:11 says: "So shall my word be that goeth forth out of my mouth: it shall not return unto me void, but it shall accomplish that which I please, and it shall prosper in the thing whereto I sent it."

Read each verse and transform it by the (WORD)

137 Righteous *art* thou, O LORD, and upright *are* thy **words**. **138** Thy
words *that* thou hast commanded *are* righteous and very faithful. **139** My
zeal hath consumed me, because mine enemies have forgotten thy **words**.
140 Thy **word** *is* very pure: therefore thy servant loveth it. **141** I *am* small
and despised: *yet* do not I forget thy **words.** **142** Thy righteousness *is* an
everlasting righteousness, and thy **word** *is* the truth. **143** Trouble and
anguish have taken hold on me: *yet* thy **words** *are* my delights. **144** The
righteousness of thy **words** *is* everlasting: give me understanding, and I
shall live.

Study Guide:
Write the words that were transformed by the Word?

1.________ 4.___________ 7.___________
2.________ 5.___________ 8.___________
3.________ 6.___________

Choose a memory verse

Psalm119:

____
____
____
____
____
____
____
____

Which verse challenged or blessed you after being transformed? Explain

____
____
____
____
____
____
____
____
____

19

KOPH

Psalms 119:145-152

Discuss / Meditate

Cry Out for God's Word

Our crying out for God Word involves Prayer which is talking to God and asking him for what we need or want for examples the two blind men in St. Matthews 20:30 cried out to be healed of their blindness. And, behold, two blind men sitting by the way side, when they heard that Jesus (the living Word) passed by, cried out, saying, Have mercy on us, O Lord, thou son of David.

Read each verse and transform it by the (WORD)

145 I cried with *my* whole heart; hear me, O LORD: I will keep thy **words.**
146 I cried unto thee; save me, and I shall keep thy **words.** **147** I prevented
the dawning of the morning, and cried: I hoped in thy **word.** **148** Mine eyes
prevent the *night* watches that I might meditate in thy **word.** **149** Hear my
voice according unto thy loving kindness: O LORD, quicken me according to thy **word**
150 They draw nigh that follow after mischief: they are far from thy **word.** **151** Thou *art*
near, O LORD; and all thy **words** *are* truth. **152** Concerning thy **words,** I have known of old
that thou hast founded them forever.

Study Guide:
Write the words that were transformed by the Word?

1.________ 4.___________ 7.___________
2.________ 5.___________ 8.___________
3.________ 6.___________

Choose a memory verse

Psalm119:

____
____
____
____
____
____
____
____

Which verse challenged or blessed you after being transformed? Explain

____
____
____
____
____
____
____
____
____

20

ר

RESH

Psalms 119:153-160

Discuss / Meditate

Keep God's Word in Adversity

One of the great examples of dealing with adversity, Can be learned in what David did when he and his men return home to Ziklag and found their families taken and their homes burned. David reveals his strength in adversity I Samuel 30:6 says, "he encouraged himself in the LORD his God: Proverb 24:10 says:" If thou faint in the day of adversity, thy strength is small."

Read each verse and transform it by the (WORD)

153 Consider mine affliction, and deliver me: for I do not forget thy **word.**
154 Plead my cause, and deliver me: quicken me according to thy **word.**
155 Salvation *is* far from the wicked: for they seek not thy **words. 156** Great *are*
thy tender mercies, O LORD: quicken me according to thy **words. 157** Many *are*
my persecutors and mine enemies; *yet* do I not decline from thy **words. 158** I
beheld the transgressors, and was grieved; because they kept not thy **word.**
159 Consider how I love thy **words** quicken me, O LORD, according to thy loving
kindness. **160** Thy **word** *is* true *from* the beginning: and every one of thy righteous
words *endureth* forever.

Study Guide:
Write the words that were transformed by the Word?

1.________ 4.___________ 7.___________
2.________ 5.___________ 8.___________
3.________ 6.___________

Choose a memory verse

Psalm119:

____
____
____
____
____
____
____
____

Which verse challenged or blessed you after being transformed? Explain

____
____
____
____
____
____
____
____
____

21

SCHIN

Psalms 119:161-168

Discuss / Meditate

Peace in Keeping God's Word

There is Peace in keeping God's Word there's: Great Peace (Psalms 119:165) there is Perfect Peace (Isaiah 26:3) "Thou wilt keep him in perfect peace, whose mind is stayed on thee: because he trusteth in thee." and there is Peace that passes understanding (Philippians 4:7) And the peace of God, which passeth all understanding, shall keep your hearts and minds through Christ Jesus.

Read each verse and transform it by the (WORD)

161 Princes have persecuted me without a cause: but my heart standeth in awe of
thy **word.** **162** I rejoice at thy **word,** as one that findeth great spoil. **163** I hate and
abhor lying: *but* thy **word** do I love. **164** Seven times a day do I praise thee
because of thy righteous **words.** **165** Great peace has they that love thy word and
nothing shall offend them. **166** LORD, I have hoped for thy salvation, and done thy
words. **167** My soul hath kept thy **words;** and I love them exceedingly. **168** I have
kept thy **words** and thy testimonies: for all my **words** *are* before thee.

Study Guide:

Write the words that were transformed by the Word?

1.________ 4.__________ 7.__________
2.________ 5.__________ 8.__________
3.________ 6.__________

Choose a memory verse

Psalm119:

____
____
____
____
____
____
____
____

Which verse challenged or blessed you after being transformed? Explain

____
____
____
____
____
____
____
____
____

22

ת

TAV

Psalms 119:169-176

Discuss / Meditate

Pray for God's Word of Understanding

Paul prayed for God's Word of understanding for the Ephesians Churches: "That the God of our Lord Jesus Christ, the Father of glory, may give unto you the spirit of wisdom and revelation in the knowledge of him: The eyes of your understanding being enlightened; that ye may know what is the hope of his calling, and what the riches of the glory of his inheritance in the saints," Ephesians 1:17-18

Read each verse and transform it by the (WORD)

169 Let my cry come near before thee, O LORD: give me understanding according
to thy **word.** **170** Let my supplication come before thee: deliver me according to
thy **word.** **171** My lips shall utter praise, when thou hast taught me thy **words.**
172 My tongue shall speak of thy **word:** for all thy words *are* righteousness.
173 Let thine hand help me; for I have chosen thy **words.****174** I have longed for thy
salvation, O LORD; and thy **word** *is* my delight. **175** Let my soul live, and it shall
praise thee; and let thy words help me. **176** I have gone astray like a lost sheep;
seek thy servant; for I do not forget thy **words.**

Study Guide:
Write the words that were transformed by the Word?

1.________	4.___________	7.___________
2.________	5.___________	8.___________
3.________	6.___________	

Choose a memory verse

Psalm119:

____
____
____
____
____
____
____
____

Which verse challenged or blessed you after being transformed? Explain

____
____
____
____
____
____
____
____
____

TRANSFORMED BY THE LIVING WORD

The word of God is alive whether it's spoken or written, Hebrews 4:12 reads "For the word of God *is* quick, and powerful, and sharper than any two edged sword, piercing even to the dividing asunder of soul and spirit, and of the joints and marrow, and *is* a discerner of the thoughts and intents of the heart." The word quick can be translated alive. The word of God is alive and gives life. The great mystery and miracle is that the Word of God became flesh, a human, a man says St. John 1:14: "And the Word was made flesh, and dwelt among us, (and we beheld his glory, the glory as of the only begotten of the Father,) full of grace and truth." The living Word of God is what gives life to all things St. John 1:3 reads "and all things were made by him and without him was not anything made that was made" Hebrews 11:3 says "Through faith we understand that the worlds were framed by the word of God, so that things which are seen were not made of things which do appear." The Word of God in the person of Jesus Christ came into the world in human form born of the virgin, Mary, and was proclaimed to be the Son of God by an angel Luke 1:35 reads: And the angel answered and said unto her, The Holy Ghost shall come upon thee, and the power of the Highest shall overshadow thee: therefore also that holy thing which shall be born of thee shall be called the Son of God.

I John 1:1-4 declares: "That which was from the beginning, which we have heard, which we have seen with our eyes, which we have looked upon, and our hands have handled, of the Word of life; (For the life was manifested, and we have seen *it*, and bear witness, and show unto you that eternal life, which was with the Father, and was manifested unto us;) That which we have seen and heard declare we unto you, that ye also may have fellowship with us: and truly our fellowship *is* with the Father, and with his Son Jesus Christ. And these things write we unto you, that your joy may be full."

The Apostle John gives us blessed assurance that he and those who were with him saw, heard and touched Jesus before and after his resurrection and promises that if we would believe him our joy would be full. *God knows mine is!* Remember what Jesus said to Thomas and the other disciples after his resurrection he said, "you believe because you have seen me but blessed are they who have not seen and yet have believed." Praise God! As my friend and Pastor the late James Lennox would sing. "I'm one of them today". I believe Jesus the living Word can change anything or anybody."

Jesus first recorded miracle was transforming water into wine, he transformed a boy's lunch into a meal for over five thousand men, women and children. He transformed a fish into ATM machine so Peter could pay their taxes. He transformed unstable waters into a watery escalator. He transformed the blind to see the dumb to talk and the lame to walk he transformed the demon possessed out of his mind man to being clothe and in his right mind. He transforms unbelievers into believers. He spoke to stormy winds and hurricane waters saying peace be still and they obey his voice. This he did and so much more reads John 21:25 "And there are also many other things which Jesus did, the which, if they should be written every one, I suppose that even the world itself could not contain the books that should be written. Amen." Yes the living Word of God did great and mighty miracles, but none of that made a difference in mankind's eternal destiny. There was but one way for man to be transformed from death to life. And that way was for a man to live a sinless life and be willing to sacrifice his sinless life for the sins of humanity (the devil really thought he had check mate on God). But God' had a strategy before the foundation of the world "it's what I call **Gods no fault insurance plan"** Proverbs 8:22-23 reads: "The LORD possessed me in the beginning of his way, before his works of old. I was setup from <u>everlasting</u>, from the beginning, or ever the earth was." Solomon was the one talking here but by discernment we know he was not talking about himself but was by revelation speaking of his descendent Jesus Christ. The word's" I was setup" reveal that there was a planned agreement and strategy made (when?) before the foundation of the world (for what?) to cover, protect and redeem Gods most valuable investment Man. (Satan) the prince of this world had no idea of this plan for I Corinthians 2:7-8 says: "But we speak the wisdom of God in a mystery, even the hidden wisdom, which God ordained before the world (Proverbs 8:22-23) unto our glory: Which none of the princes of this world (St. John12:31) knew (evil spirits) for had they known it, they would not have crucified the Lord of glory." What didn't they know? That by Jesus sinless life and sacrificial death, burial and resurrection he would destroy the work of Satan for all eternity Satan's work and plan was to condemn all of mankind through sin to eternal death, hell and separation from God our Father, as he and all the fallen angel's now known as demon's which were cast out of heaven with him, but I John chapter three verse eight says "For this purpose was the Son of God manifested, that he might destroy the works of the devil." I John 3:8b

John the Baptist came preached: "Behold the Lamb of God, which taketh away the sin of the world." The sin was and is always disobedience to the will of God, which is passed from Adam to every living creature, death and separation from God being the penalty. Romans 8:19-21says: "For the earnest expectation of the creature waiteth for the manifestation of the sons of God. For the creature was made subject to vanity (death), not willingly, but by reason of him who hath subjected *the same* in hope, because the creature itself also shall be delivered from the bondage of corruption (death) into the glorious liberty of the children of God." From Adam until Jesus, men lived and died and their souls went down to hell, Hades or paradise.

The scriptures I believe give a glimpse of the location of the dead before Christ transformed and translated them. The first example is the prophet Samuel who was one of the most honored and respected prophets of Old Testament. When Samuel died, King Saul was tormented by evil spirit because of his disobedience to the Lord. The scripture says, *"that the Lord wouldn't talk to him."* So he sought for a witch with a familiar spirit (a psychic) to *bring-up* Samuel, notice it doesn't say bring-down Samuel from above but the direction is *bring-up* Samuel. Samuel himself asked King Saul why he had brought *him up.* I Samuel 28:7-15 reads: Then said Saul unto his servants, Seek me a woman that hath a familiar spirit, that I may go to her, and enquire of her. And his servants said to him, Behold, *there is* a woman that hath a familiar spirit at Endor. And Saul disguised himself, and put on other raiment, and he went, and two men with him, and they came to the woman by night: and he said, I pray thee, divine unto me by the familiar spirit, and bring me *him* up, whom I shall name unto thee. And the woman said unto him, Behold, thou knowest what Saul hath done, how he hath cut off those that have familiar spirits, and the wizards, out of the land:

wherefore then layest thou a snare for my life, to cause me to die? And Saul swore to her by the LORD, saying, "*as* the LORD liveth, there shall no punishment happen to thee for this thing." Then said the woman, whom shall I bring up unto thee? And he said, bring me up Samuel. And when the woman saw Samuel, she cried with a loud voice: and the woman spoke to Saul, saying, why hast thou deceived me? For thou *art* Saul. And the king said unto her, Be not afraid: for what sawest thou? And the woman said unto Saul, I saw gods *ascending out of the earth.* And he said unto her, what form *is* he of? And she said, an old man cometh up; and he *is* covered with a mantle. And Saul perceived that it *was* Samuel, and he stooped with *his* face to the ground, and bowed himself. And Samuel said to Saul, Why hast thou disquieted me, *to bring me up?* And Saul answered, I am sore distressed; for the Philistines make war against me, and God is departed from me, and answereth me no more, neither by prophets, nor by dreams: therefore I have called thee, that thou mayest make known unto me what I shall do."

A great example also is King David who makes a profound statement about his souls resting place and the place of the Holy One, Christ, the Messiah in Psalm 15:7- 10 he says:" I will bless the LORD, who hath given me counsel: my reins also instruct me in the night seasons. I have set the LORD always before me: because *he is* at my right hand, I shall not be moved. Therefore my heart is glad, and my glory rejoiceth: my flesh also shall rest in hope. *For thou wilt not leave my soul in hell; neither wilt thou suffer thine Holy One to see corruption."*

In verse ten King David declares his belief that his soul would not be left in hell and neither would the Holy one (the Living Word Jesus) see corruption. What a powerful prophetic insight given to David to know number one that his soul would not be left in hell Hades, paradise. Samuel if you recall asked King Saul why? He had called him *up* notice the direction again that he came, Samuel came up meaning he had to come from down. The second thing he says is "neither wilt thou suffer thine Holy One to see corruption." The Holy one he spoke of I believe is Jesus the living Word.

In John 1:29b Jesus said of himself; I am the way, the truth, and the life: no man cometh unto the Father, (to Heaven) but by me. Before Jesus resurrection the scriptures record only two persons who were taken up into heaven they are Enoch (Genesis 5:24) and Elijah II Kings 2: I believe that through Jesus resurrection we are now able to be transform to live for him on earth and translated to live with him in heaven. Transformed means to be changed Romans 12:2 says," be transformed *(changed)* by the renewing of your mind and II Corinthians 5:17 reads "If any man *be* in Christ, *he is* a new creature: old things are passed away, behold, all things are becoming new" (transformed).

Translated is to be moved or repositioned the Apostle Paul said in Colossians 1:13 "that God hath delivered us from the power of darkness, and hath translated *us* into the kingdom of his dear Son" The kingdom that this verse is referring to is twofold one it speaks of the kingdom as a life style the other speaks of the kingdom as a place: The Kingdom of God being a lifestyle:" For the Kingdom of God is not meat and drink but righteousness peace and joy in the Holy Ghost" and The Kingdom of Heaven being a place: Jesus spoke about the place in John 14:2-3"I go to prepare a place for you. And if I go and prepare a place for you, I will come again, and receive you unto myself; that where I am, *there* ye may be also."

King David foresaw this translation and prophesied saying:" thou wilt not leave my soul in hell; neither wilt thou suffer (allow) thine Holy One (Jesus) to see corruption." (Psalms 16:10) Jesus and one of the two thieves who died on the crosses with him in Luke 23:40-43 it said: But the other answering rebuked him, saying, "Dost not thou fear God, seeing thou art in the same condemnation? We indeed justly, for we receive the due reward of our deeds: but this man hath done nothing amiss. And he said unto Jesus, Lord, remember me when thou cometh into thy kingdom." "And Jesus said unto him, "Verily I say unto thee, today shalt thou be with me in *paradise.*" In other words Jesus was saying to this man; today I will take you with me into paradise. Paradise being the place where Abraham, Isaac and Jacob were; along with all those who die in hope, the hope that David prophesied of in Psalm 16:10." Thou will not leave my soul in hell neither wilt thou suffer thine Holy One to see corruption.

Lastly, Jesus tells the story of the rich man and the poor man Lazarus, how the rich man went to hell and was in torment but Lazarus went to paradise and was laying in Abraham's bosom. St. Luke 16:19-26 There was a certain rich man, which was clothed in purple and fine linen, and fared sumptuously every day: And there was a certain beggar named Lazarus, which was laid at his gate, full of sores, And desiring to be fed with the crumbs which fell from the rich man's table: moreover the dogs came and licked his sores. And it came to pass, that the beggar died, and was carried by the angels into Abraham's bosom: the rich man also died, and was buried.

And in hell he lifts up his eyes, being in torments, and seeth Abraham afar off, and Lazarus in his bosom. And he cried and said, Father Abraham, have mercy on me, and send Lazarus, that he may dip the tip of his finger in water, and cool my tongue, for I am tormented in this flame. But Abraham said, Son, remember that thou in thy lifetime receivest thy good things, and likewise Lazarus evil things: but now he is comforted, and thou art tormented. And beside all this, between you, and us there is a great gulf fixed: so that they, which would pass from hence to you, cannot; neither can they pass to us that would come from thence. Then he said, I pray thee therefore, father, that thou wouldest send him to my father's house: For I have five brethren; that he may testify unto them, lest they also come into this place of torment. Abraham saith unto him, they have Moses and the prophets; let them hear them. And he said, Nay, father Abraham: but if one went unto them from the dead, they will repent. And he said unto him, if they hear not Moses and the prophets, neither would they be persuaded, though one rose from the dead.

I believe when Jesus the living Word die on the cross and gave up the ghost (Luke 23:46) and was buried in Joseph of Arimathaea tomb; that when they rolled the rock over the opening of that grave immediately Jesus spirit stepped back into his body and went down into paradise and for three day and three night he preach but on the third day he rose and translate the church of the pass into heaven above according to Ephesians 4:8-10 which says: When he ascended up on high, he led captivity captive, and gave gifts unto men. (Now that he ascended, what is it but that he also descended *first* into the lower parts of the earth? He that descended is the same also that ascended up far above all heavens, that he might fill all things.) He ascended to the place he'd promised the disciples he was going to prepare for them and the church of the future as John 14:1-6 tells us: Let not your heart be troubled: ye believe in God, believe also in me. In my Father's house are many mansions: if it were not so, I would have told you. I go to prepare a place for you. And if I go and prepare a place for you, I will come again, and receive you unto myself; that where I am, there ye may be also. And whither I go ye know, and the way ye know. Thomas saith unto him, Lord, we know not whither thou goest; and how can we know the way? Jesus saith unto him, I am the way, the truth, and the life: no man cometh unto the Father, but by me. .

When he ascended up on high (to heaven) he didn't go alone the scripture say he led captivity captive the captivity was those such as Adam and Eve, Abraham, Isaac and Jacob, Noah and King David, John the Baptist etc. etc. Oh and let's not forget the thief on the cross whom Jesus promised that; this day he would be with him in paradise.

The Living Word opened the door to no more separation between God and man. The Apostle Paul says to be absent from the body is to be present with the LORD (II Corinthians 5:8). Jesus the living Word is the only man in heaven now with a glorified body. But according to I John 3:2 we will be like him (having glorified bodies when the rapture takes place The Apostle Paul says in: I Corinthians 15:51-52 that "Behold, I show you a mystery; We shall not all sleep, but we shall all be changed, In a moment, in the twinkling of an eye, at the last trump: for the trumpet shall sound, and the dead shall be raised incorruptible, and we shall be changed."

In I Thessalonians 4:16-18 he says: "For the Lord himself shall descend from heaven with a shout, with the voice of the archangel, and with the trump of God: and the dead in Christ shall rise first: Then we which are alive and remain shall be caught up together with them in the clouds, to meet the Lord in the air: and so shall we ever be with the Lord. Wherefore comfort one another with these words."

The living Word is coming back again for them that are looking for him to transform and translate them to they're heavenly home. (Hebrews 9:28)

The spoken Word transformed into the written Word and the written Word transformed into the living Word and the living Word translated itself back to heaven and into the hearts of all who will receive him. Amen.

Meditation Scriptures On the Living Word

1. St. John6:51, I am the living bread, which came down from heaven: if any man eats of this bread, he shall live forever: and the bread that I will give is my flesh, which I will give for the life of the world.

2. St. John 10:10, the thief cometh not, but for to steal, and to kill, and to destroy: I am come that they might have life, and that they might have it more abundantly.

3. St. John 5:26 For as the Father hath life in himself; so hath he given to the Son to have life in himself;

4. St. John 4:14 But whosoever drinketh of the water that I shall give him shall never thirst; but the water that I shall give him shall be in him a well of water springing up into everlasting life.

5. St. John 14:6 Jesus saith unto him, I am the way, the truth, and the life: no man cometh unto the Father, but by me.

Psalm 119:1-176

TRANSFORMED BY THE WORD KJV

ALEPH

1 Blessed are the undefiled in the way, who walk in the law of the LORD.

2 Blessed are they that keep his testimonies, and that seek him with the whole heart.

3 They also do no iniquity: they walk in his ways.

4 Thou hast commanded us to keep thy precepts diligently.

5 O that my words were directed to keep thy statutes!

6 Then shall I not be ashamed, when I have respect unto all thy commandments.

7 I will praise thee with uprightness of heart, when I shall have learned thy righteous judgments.

8 I will keep thy statutes: O forsakes me not utterly.

BETH

9 Wherewithal shall a young man cleanse his way? By taking heed thereto according to thy word.

10 With my whole heart have I sought thee: O let me not wander from thy commandments.

11 Thy word have I hid in mine heart, that I might not sin against thee.

12 Blessed art thou, O LORD: teach me thy statutes.

13 With my lips have I declared all the judgments of thy mouth?

14 I have rejoiced in the way of thy testimonies, as much as in all riches.

15 I will meditate in thy precepts, and have respect unto thy ways.

16 I will delight myself in thy statues: I will not forget thy word.

GIMEL

17 Deal bountifully with thy servant, that I may live, and keep thy word.

18 Open thou mine eyes, that I may behold wondrous things out of thy law.

19 I am a stranger in the earth: hide not thy commandments from me.

20 My soul breaketh for the longing that it hath unto thy judgments at all times.

21 Thou hast rebuked the proud that are cursed, which do err from thy commandments.

22 Remove from me reproach and contempt, for I have kept thy testimonies.

23 Princes also did sit and speak against me: but thy servant did meditate in thy statutes.

24 Thy testimonies also are my delight and my counselors.

DALETH

25 My soul cleaveth unto the dust: quicken thou me according to thy word.

26 I have declared my words, and thou heardest me: teach me thy statues.

27 Make me to understand the way of thy precepts: so shall I talk of thy wondrous works.

28 My soul melteth for heaviness: strengthen thou me according unto thy word.

29 Remove from me the way of lying: and grant me thy law graciously.

30 I have chosen the way of truth: thy judgments have I laid before me.

31 I have stuck unto thy testimonies: O LORD, put me not to shame.

32 I will run the way of thy commandments, when thou shalt enlarge my heart.

HE

33 Teach me, O LORD, the way of thy statues; and I shall keep it unto the end.

34 Give me understanding, and I shall keep thy law; yea, I shall observe it with my whole heart.

35 Make me to go in the path of thy commandments, for therein do I delight.

36 Incline my heart unto thy testimonies, and not to covetousness.

37 Turn away mine eyes from beholding vanity; and quicken thou me in thy way.

38 Establish thy word unto thy servant, who is devoted to thy fear.

39 Turn away my reproach, which I fear: for thy judgments are good.

40 Behold, I have longed after thy precepts: quicken me in thy righteousness.

VAV

41 Let thy mercies come also unto me, O LORD, even thy salvation, according to thy word.

42 So shall I have wherewith to answer him that reproacheth me: for I trust in thy word.

43 And take not the word of truth utterly out of my mouth, for I have hoped in thy judgments.

44 So shall I keep thy law continually forever and ever.

45 And I will walk at liberty: for I seek thy precepts.

46 I will speak of thy testimonies also before kings, and will not be ashamed.

47 And I will delight myself in thy commandments, which I have loved.

48 My hands also will I lift up unto thy commandments, which I have loved; and I will meditate in thy statues.

ZAYIN

49 Remember the word unto thy servant, upon which thou hast caused me to hope.

50 This is my comfort in my affliction: for thy word hath quickened me.

51 The proud have had me greatly in derision: yet have I not declined from thy law.

52 I remembered thy judgments of old, O LORD; and have comforted myself.

53 Horror hath taken hold upon me because of the wicked that forsake thy law.

54 Thy statues have been my songs in the house of my pilgrimage.

55 I have remembered thy name, O LORD, in the night, and have kept thy law.

56 This I had, because I kept thy precepts.

CHETH

57 Thou art my portion, O LORD: I have said that I would keep thy words.

58 I entreated thy favour with my whole heart: be merciful unto me according to thy word.

59 I thought on my ways, and turned my feet unto thy testimonies.

60 I made haste, and delayed not to keep thy commandments.

61 The bands of the wicked have robbed me: but I have not forgotten thy law.

62 At midnight I will rise to give thanks unto thee because of thy righteous judgments.

63 I am a companion of all them that fear thee, and of them that keep thy precepts.

64 The earth, O LORD, is full of thy mercy: teach me thy statues.

TETH

65 Thou hast dealt well with thy servant, O LORD, according unto thy word.

66 Teach me good judgment and knowledge: for I have believed thy commandments.

67 Before I was afflicted I went astray: but now have I kept thy word.

68 Thou art good, and doest good; teach me thy statues.

69 The proud have forged a lie against me: but I will keep thy precepts with my whole heart.

70 Their heart is as fat as grease; but I delight in thy law.

71 It is good for me that I have been afflicted; that I might learn thy statues.

72 The law of thy mouth is better unto me than thousands of gold and silver.

YOD

73 Thy hands have made me and fashioned me: give me understanding, that I may learn thy commandments.

74 They that fear thee will be glad when they see me because I have hoped in thy word.

75 I know, O LORD, that thy judgments are right, and that thou in faithfulness hast afflicted me.

76 Let, I pray thee, thy merciful kindness be for my comfort, according to thy word unto thy servant.

77 Let thy tender mercies come unto me, that I may live: for thy law is my delight.

78 Let the proud be ashamed; for they dealt perversely with me without a cause: but I will meditate in thy precepts.

79 Let those that fear thee turn unto me, and those that have known thy testimonies.

80 Let my heart be sound in thy statues; that I be not ashamed.

CAPH

81 My soul fainteth for thy salvation: but I hope in thy word.

82 Mine eyes fail for thy word, saying, When wilt thou comfort me?

83 For I am become like a bottle in the smoke, yet do I not forget thy statues?

84 How many are the days of thy servant? When wilt thou execute judgment on them that persecute me?

85 The proud have dug pits for me, which are not after thy law.

86 All thy commandments are faithful: they persecute me wrongfully; help thou me.

87 They had almost consumed me upon earth; but I forsook not thy precepts.

88 Quicken me after thy loving kindness; so shall I keep the testimony of thy mouth.

LAMED

89 Forever, O LORD, thy word is settled in heaven.

90 Thy faithfulness is unto all generations: thou hast established the earth, and it abideth.

91 They continue this day according to thine ordinances: for all are thy servants.

92 Unless thy law had been my delights, I should then have perished in mine affliction.

93 I will never forget thy precepts: for with them thou hast quickened me.

94 I am thine, save me for I have sought thy precepts.

95 The wicked have waited for me to destroy me: but I will consider thy testimonies.

96 I have seen an end of all perfection: but thy commandment is exceeding broad.

MEM

97 O how love I thy law! It is my meditation all the day.

98 Thou through thy commandments hast made me wiser than mine enemies: for they are ever with me.

99 I have more understanding than all my teachers: for thy testimonies are my meditation.

100 I understand more than the ancients, because I keep thy precepts.

101 I have refrained my feet from every evil way, that I might keep thy word.

102 I have not departed from thy judgments: for thou hast taught me.

103 How sweet are thy words unto my taste! Yea, sweeter than honey to my mouth!

104 Through thy precepts I get understanding: therefore I hate every false way.

NUN

105 Thy word is a lamp unto my feet, and a light unto my path.

106 I have sworn, and I will perform it, that I will keep thy righteous judgments.

107 I am afflicted very much: quicken me, O LORD, according unto thy word.

108 Accept, I beseech thee, the freewill offerings of my mouth, O LORD, and teach me thy judgments.

109 My soul is continually in my hand: yet do I not forget thy law.

110 The wicked have laid a snare for me: yet I erred not from thy precepts.

111 Thy testimonies have I taken as a heritage forever: for they are the rejoicing of my heart.

112 I have inclined mine heart to perform thy statues always, even unto the end.

SAMECH

113 I hate vain thoughts: but thy word do I love.

114 Thou art my hiding place and my shield: I hope in thy word.

115 Depart from me, ye evildoers: for I will keep the commandments of my God.

116 Uphold me according unto thy word that I may live: and let me not be ashamed of my hope.

117 Hold thou me up, and I shall be safe: and I will have respect unto thy statues continually.

118 Thou hast trodden down all them that err from thy statues: for their deceit is falsehood.

119 Thou putteth away all the wicked of the earth like dross: therefore I love thy testimonies.

120 My flesh trembleth for fear of thee; and I am afraid of thy judgments.

AIN

121 I have done judgment and justice: leave me not to mine oppressors.

122 Be surety for thy servant for good: let not the proud oppress me.

123 Mine eyes fail for thy salvation, and for the word of thy righteousness.

124 Deal with thy servant according unto thy mercy, and teach me thy statues.

125 I am thy servant; give me understanding, that I may know thy testimonies.

126 It is time for thee, LORD, to work: for they have made void thy law.

127 Therefore I love thy commandments above gold, yea, above fine gold.

128 Therefore I esteem all thy precepts concerning all things to be right; and I hate every false way.

PE

129 Thy testimonies are wonderful: therefore doth my soul keep them.

130 The entrance of thy words giveth light; it giveth understanding unto the simple.

131 I opened my mouth, and panted: for I longed for thy commandments.

132 Look thou upon me, and be merciful unto me, as thou usest to do unto those that love thy name.

133 Order my steps in thy word: and let not any iniquity have dominion over me.

134 Deliver me from the oppression of man: so will I keep thy precepts.

135 Make thy face to shine upon thy servant; and teach me thy statues.

136 Rivers of waters run down mine eyes, because they keep not thy law.

TZADDI

137 Righteous art thou, O LORD, and upright are thy judgments.

138 Thy testimonies that thou hast commanded are righteous and very faithful.

139 My zeal hath consumed me, because mine enemies have forgotten thy words.

140 Thy word is very pure: therefore thy servant loveth it.

141 I am small and despised: yet do not I forget thy precepts.

142 Thy righteousness is an everlasting righteousness, and thy law is the truth.

143 Trouble and anguish have taken hold on me: yet thy commandments are my delights.

144 The righteousness of thy testimonies is everlasting: give me understanding, and I shall live.

KOPH

145 I cried with my whole heart, hear me, O LORD: I will keep thy statues.

146 I cried unto thee; save me, and I shall keep thy testimonies.

147 I prevented the dawning of the morning, and cried: I hoped in thy word.

148 Mine eyes prevent the night watches that I might meditate in thy word.

149 Hear my voice according unto thy loving kindness: O LORD, quicken me according to thy judgment.

150 They draw nigh that follow after mischief: they are far from thy law.

151 Thou art near, O LORD; and all thy commandments are truth.

152 Concerning thy testimonies, I have known of old that thou hast founded them forever.

RESH

Consider mine affliction, and deliver me: for I do not forget thy law.
153

154 Plead my cause, and deliver me: quicken me according to thy word.

155 Salvation is far from the wicked: for they seek not thy statues.

156 Great are thy tender mercies, O LORD: quicken me according to thy judgments.

157 Many are my persecutors and mine enemies; yet do I not decline from thy testimonies.

158 I beheld the transgressors, and was grieved because they kept not thy word.

159 Consider how I love thy precepts: quicken me, O LORD, according to thy loving kindness.

160 Thy word is true from the beginning: and every one of thy righteous judgments endureth forever.

SCHIN

161 Princes have persecuted me without a cause: but my heart standeth in awe of thy word.

162 I rejoice at thy word, as one that findeth great spoil.

163 I hate and abhor lying: but thy law do I love.

164 Seven times a day do I praise thee because of thy righteous judgments?

165 Great peace has they, which love thy law: and nothing shall offend them.

166 LORD, I have hoped for thy salvation, and done thy commandments.

167 My soul hath kept thy testimonies; and I love them exceedingly.

168 I have kept thy precepts and thy testimonies: for all my ways are before thee.

TAV

169 Let my cry come near before thee, O LORD: give me understanding according to thy word.

170 Let my supplication come before thee: deliver me according to thy word.

171 My lips shall utter praise, when thou hast taught me thy statutes.

172 My tongue shall speak of thy word: for all thy commandments are righteousness.

173 Let thine hand help me, for I have chosen thy precepts.

174 I have longed for thy salvation, O LORD; and thy law is my delight.

175 Let my soul live, and it shall praise thee; and let thy judgment help me.

176 I have gone astray like a lost sheep; seek thy servant, for I do not forget thy commandments.

A Brief Definition of Each Hebrew Letters and their Numeric Values

1. א **(Aleph)** meaning Strenght;the numerical value is One
2. ב **(Beth)** meaning House;the numerical value is Two
3. ג **(Gimel)** meaning Foot;the numerical value is Three
4. ד **(Daleth)** meaning Door;the numerical value is Four
5. ה (He) meaning Give and Receive;the numerical value is Five
6. ו **(Vav)** meaning Man standing;the numerical value is Six
7. ז **(Zayin)** meaning Crown; the numerical value is Seven
8. ח **(Cheth)** meaning Gateway; the numerical value is Eight
9. ט **(Teth)** meaning Vessel; the numerical value is Nine
10. י **(Yod)** meaning Hand; the numerical value is Ten
11. כ ך **(Caph)** meaning Potential; the numerical value is Twenty
12. ל **(Lamed)** meaning Learn to Teach; the numerical value is Thirty
13. מ ם **(Mem)** meaning Water;the numerical value is Forty
14. נ ן **(Nun)** meaning Faithful Servent; the numerical value is Fifty
15. **(Samech)** meaning Surround; the numerical value is Sixty

16. ע **(Ain)** meaning Eye;the numerical value is Seventy

17. פ ף **(Pe)** meaning mouth; the numerical value is Eighty

18. צ ץ **(Tzaddi)** meaning rightious one; the numerical is Ninety

19. ק **(Koph)** meaning going down; the numerical value is One Hundred

20. ר **(Resh)** meaning Head; the numerical value is Two Hundred

שׂ

21. שׁ **(Schin)** meaning Fire; the numerical value is Three Hundred

22. ת **(Tav)** meaning Seal; the numerical value is Four Hundred

ABOUT THE AUTHOR

Pastor Willie F. Richardson has been preaching the gospel of Jesus Christ for over forty years. He is the founding pastor of the Bread of Life Church in Chicago, IL for over 27 years. He is the proud father of four children, eight grandchildren, and four great grandchildren. Last but not least he has been married to the love of his life Donsella for 50 years on November 15, 2020.

www.ingramcontent.com/pod-product-compliance
Lightning Source LLC
LaVergne TN
LVHW050938080826
845145LV00004B/1316

* 9 7 8 0 5 7 8 1 7 1 4 3 2 *